The Science of Goodbyes

The Science of Goodbyes

POEMS BY
MYRA SKLAREW

Athens
The University of Georgia Press

Copyright © 1982 by the University of Georgia Press
Athens, Georgia 30602

All rights reserved

Set in 10 on 12 point Monticello type
Printed in the United States of America

Library of Congress Cataloging in Publication Data

Sklarew, Myra.
   The science of goodbyes.

   I. Title.
PS3569.K57S35   811'.54   81-16023
ISBN 0-8203-0603-7   AACR2
ISBN 0-8203-0604-5 (pbk.)

I have studied the science of goodbyes . . .

—OSIP MANDELSTAM

Acknowledgments

Acknowledgment is given to the following publications in which poems from this book first appeared.

Black Box Magazine: "Letting the Plants Die"
Carolina Quarterly: "In Bed"
Chowder Review: "Blessed Art Thou, No-One"
Forum: "After Theresienstadt"
Maariv: "Poem of the Mother," "Sacrifice," translated by the Israeli poet Moshe Dor
Moment: "A Three-Course Meal for the New Year"
National Jewish Monthly: "Instructions for the Messiah"
New Jersey Poetry Journal: "Appeasing a River"
The New York Times: "My Daughter's Dream," "Hostage," "Marriage," "The Town"
Poet Lore: "If You Are Willing," "The Traveler," "Winter Solstice," "Exchange," "For This," "Leaving"
Quest/79: "Poem of the Mother"
Response: "A Worthy Cause"
Visions: "Twenty-four Hours"
Washington Dossier: "The Way the World Is"
Window: "Insomnia," "August"

I should like to acknowledge anthologies in which some of these poems appeared: *City Celebration 1976, The Ear's Chamber, The Poet Upstairs, Rye Bread, Second Rising, Voices Within the Ark*. The poem "Decision" was used in a Bicentennial Photography and Poetry Exhibit, Martin Luther King Library, Washington, D.C. "Somnambulist" received the Gordon Barber Award from the Poetry Society of America. Portions of this collection have also been recorded for the Library of Congress' Contemporary Poets Series.

To these, to Charley and Pam Plymell of *Cherry Valley Editions*, publishers of *In the Basket of the Blind*, to Ron Slate of *Chowder Chapbooks* for poems which appeared in a chapbook entitled *Blessed Art Thou, No-One*, to Merrill Leffler of Dryad Press, to friends who share this life with me, I thank you.

M.S.

Deborah and Eric

For you, my blessings

Contents

I

The Leaving

Somnambulist

1

This morning
while I slept,
Barba-Yiorgos,
you left
one brown egg
and a saucepan
of goat's milk
on the kitchen table.

Between the hen
and her egg
on my table
there is only
the small distance
between your house
and mine.

But what
shall I bring
for you, Barba-Yiorgos?
The almonds
on my tree
are also
on yours.
The white mulberries
are on both
our trees.

In the evening
you tell Nicos
that the great sea

of your passion
has turned to yoghurt
and all the small spoons
have departed.

2

When you are alone in the mountain
you may wear time on your finger
as you would a ring or you may call it
and it will walk along your arm
like a pet bird. Or you may strike time
as you would the tongue of a bell
against its hollow and there will be
more of it.

In the morning when you see small gatherings
of dust, it will only be time that the hands
of the clocks have pushed to the surface
during the night. In this way have the seconds
passed through our dreams.

The first blue light of morning descends
to earth in great crystalline chunks
also carved by tools held in hands. Five
o'clock measured in the language of bells.
Even the rain is molded by that spirit
which wrestled with the dark. Large tears
of the pietà falling to the red tiles.

3

Perhaps I am only dreaming this town
at the edge of a crater. Splinters

of my love broken into the hearts
of many others. Silence divided
by the bells marking the places of goats
here and there in the mountain. The sense
that you are there hovering in the doorway

or there in the field below or that it
was you in the dark this morning, the sound
of the hoofs of your mare on the stone
of the mountain. What shall I look for
among the groves and dim fences?
In the dooryards and spring places?

When you left, afterward I went on alone,
deeper into my life, full of the years
which had accumulated in me. When you left
I went on, along these nets of silence
like one who starts out at the
beginning when the way is narrow
and the road first opening.

Leaving

His Song

I go out foraging against
the molten core rising
rising daily inside me

against the voice saying
What did you mean to be in your life?

against the slow thought
that would come
when I drove out
on a Sunday

Ways I could change my life

But this other
this danger is too compelling
I tell you I'd die for it
The threat
of that man
with his sack of evidence
with his knife out after me
in the dark
slashing my tires
to keep me
from running off
with his wife

It doesn't matter now
It's what I want

My whole life is back there
leaning against the porch rail
thinking itself down
along the narrow edge
of the years

But it's not strong enough
to keep back
what's broken through

that part of me I set onto another
never quite fitting

It's something I can't do without
that friction to raise up a feeling
against the questions
that won't leave me
against the answer
out there in front of me

Her Song

After he left
I posted innocence
at my door

When he spoke
of his reason for leaving
I knew my own part in it
but I never said a word

At first it was good
filling up the boxes
with his books of naked girls
putting them
by the front door

7

But then
there was the empty closet
a white pill
on the floor
in the corner
the familiar smell

At night
innocence
like the book beside me
brings no comfort at all

nor the thin legs
of self-righteousness

nor the stem and leaf
of selfhood

Why is it
in my dream
it seems perfectly natural
to be taking off my clothes
in front of two men
who are naked

Perfectly natural for one
of the men to enter me
until I become aware
of someone else
standing in the corner
of that room

Hostage

You held me
tightly at first
for it was in my nature
to try to escape.

When the marks
of your fingers
grew visible
along my forearms,

when there was hidden
in your eyes
the shape of my face,
you held me off

like the head of a snake.
I grew dangerous—
skyscraper in the small room
of confinement.

When you looked down
at your own locked fingers
I was still there
as I have been from the first,

free as any life, delicate,
still breathing.

The Listening Room

You have suffered
a loss of space. There is room here
only for the apple—fixed object,
squatter in the room with a single window,
taking up all the light.

The apple makes its position clear,
bestowing its blessing while it speaks
the inaudible warning by which
you are meant to save yourself.
You are the stethoscope

pressed to its skin.
Apple: flesh of your hunger,
symptom of your fall,
landlord
and tenant in the bright room.

Decision

I have decided to continue with my life
at least for today.

After all, someone is needed to put on the coffee,
to unpack a box or trim a rug, to say a prayer

for the dead, someone to prepare the evening meal
or tie the child's shoelaces.

Someone is needed with a foothold in this year
to stand at the door of the year just gone.

I have decided to cross the threshold of my house,
to step into the new air, erasing the careful room

which I fold around myself like a shawl, erasing
the black cat who has come to fill the empty space

in order to complete the composition,
erasing the plants which bend on the mantel

like land mine detectors
in their continual search for water.

II

The Way It Is

The Dogs Are Barking

What they know of me
they will have to invent:
I wear my garments
close to my skin

They work their tongues
mounting this violation
of my empty house:
I go away inside
I go to the moon

Outside
the trees press
their naked seeds
into the air
one by one

Everywhere
there is the lesson
of nakedness

I hold to my clothing
thin as it is:
I wrap myself
in a secret cloth

Everywhere
the dogs are barking

Some claim
in a shrill voice
to have found God
I am not yet convinced

Everywhere the dogs
are barking
but the slack
in the silence
is not exhausted
and no gods
appear at my door

In the Event of a National Disaster

This
is the border
between here
and now,
between what is said
and what is meant,
between practice
and theory.

Your safe passage
is denied.

The guard
on the border
carries
a basket of eggs
about to hatch
for the hunger
of the next
generation.

He carries a white flag
in the event of your surrender.

On the border
there are many
mechanical devices: sleds
with golden runners,
the wings of fallen angels,
half-hearted wheels

with spokes bowed out,
pulleys and axles.

Everything you could possibly need
for starting up the world again.

A Worthy Cause

I rise
in the dark

my dreams done
with their thumbing
through the yellow pages
of my body's directory

I lift your sweater from Jerusalem
and fold it
and put it on the chair
I take a thread and needle
and sew the torn belt loop
I had noticed
as I bent over you
at evening

I lift your sock from Tel Aviv
your poor shoe covered with the dust
and fine bone of Masada
a grain of desert sand
sticking to the sole
copper sulfate from the Dead Sea

A little stitching
on behalf of Israel
a little mending
and folding
for our brethren in Israel

As you can see
I make my contribution

Twenty-four Hours

I had twenty-four
hours
to erase
from your body
the crust
of this world.

Chaval, Pity, you said
and we unwrapped
each other

like unlacing
the threads
which bind together
the pages of a book,

our hands touching
and going away again

like touching a town
on the map
in the morning
and then being there
at nightfall.

Love

What of these two souls
coupling and uncoupling like trains,
the metaphysics of incompletion
revitalized by the sudden union.

Let us praise isolation and longing;
let us praise the woman who talks
to herself, the young man walking
alone at night, the hand which reached out
and came upon emptiness.

Let us say a word
for the one lying next
to the other
who cannot even then name his need.

Marriage

Marriage is like that, you know—
two fine folks seated comfortably
in their used Ford motor car
sinking calmly into the sea for years
knowing how they will rise again
separately through water.

Reconciliation

Between nations
reconciliation
is easier:
old treacheries persist
dull as toothaches
or they are dispensed
a teaspoon at a time.

A border is shifted
severing a mountain
or spilling out
the contents of a lake.

A refugee
without taking a step
is transformed
to a full citizen,
a partisan
to chancellor.

Waterways are opened
letting the small ships
sail out again,
their flags
high on the mast.

Between men and women
reconciliation
is difficult, trust
uncomfortable
as a pair of new shoes.

Objects
which once inhabited
the same space
are wedged apart—jagged lines
in place for life.
Broadsheet
where there once
was book.
Who could put
these pages
together again.

Among the nations
it is decreed
that the names
of the streets
shall be changed,
the towns occupied
by new mayors,
headstones erased
in the cemetery.

The leaf
shall be driven back
to its tree;
the dismembered arm
to its socket.
The memory
of the nations
does not know
the way to us.

The Way the World Is

The husbands come back to the deserted wives
They come back from their wanderings
from Circe and her sisters
They come back through the fields through fire
through the air above
to the marriage beds lined up
in the streets and avenues
and country roads of this world

The sons forever setting out
do not recognize the fathers
whom they pass along the way
making it easier for the murders
to take place making betrayal easier

The wives standing by the kitchen doors
in their aprons with their watering cans
their jars with their bread baking in the oven
their holy days lined up like shoes their packets
of good deeds spread out on the table
The wives are missing from the cities of windows
the doors of all the houses are standing open
They have fled

III

Because I Am a Woman

Because I Am a Woman

1

Because I am a woman I do not own
this world. I write about small things,
the way the moon rounding the corner
of my house each night rose inside me
for nine months. I write of the way
a branch points to the belt of a man
towering above me in his dark house.

I seldom mention Rome nor do I own the sea
or history or my language, but I poke
in the ashes of old words like a finger
sorting through the basket of buttons.
Until recently I did not mention blood
or my body.

Perhaps a woman wrote such things
on parchment long ago, charred remnants
all that is left of that ancient library
at Alexandria, its nine hundred years'
accumulation fuel for the public baths.
Who can say for certain?

For Ataturk it was easy to obliterate
the past: he merely contented himself
with changing the alphabet, putting it
out of currency.

2

In my own time the voices of language
were sealed off in boxcars and barracks,
sound broken in midcry like bits of teeth
falling in slow motion down the throat
or breaking against air, parts of a cry.

Because I am a woman I leave
these brackish odds and ends
where they are: I go about my business.
Four nuns walking in the shadow
of stones, identical black shoes
along the narrow trail.

Or a camera on a tripod,
water hurrying on its way.
Something seen and something
hidden. Married to this world
and the one to come.

3

I did not know I was looking
for you, my sister, in these ruins.
I took what I could find, the face
of my mother with the news
of the death camps written
in blood webs across her eyes.

I take the words a man wrote:
Forget about us, about our
generation. We have envied plants
and stones, we envied dogs.

Sometimes I lie down
in a borrowed bed and sleep
for awhile. Then you, my brother,
drop anchor alongside me, starting
up the air between us. Spoke
of a wheel, hairspring, current.

4

The ancients lighted small fires
on the mountain tops from the Mount
of Olives to Babylonia until it
appeared that the whole world
was ablaze. In this way did the new
month begin. I tear off one page
of the calendar. I peel onions,
I sharpen a knife.

At night I wash myself of this world
in the language of small things:
a cup of milk cold as March
on my table, a few coins I set down
on the drainboard in the kitchen,
emptying my purse the way the dream
is emptied of its contents each morning.
History is mortgaged, death in escrow.
At night I take off my watch.

5

Once I lived in a corner
of the house, a bead on a string.
The men gathered to speak
of science and politics behind
great wooden doors. Perhaps,
I used to think, if I were older.
Perhaps if I were a boy.

My middle name was Aaron.
The priest with the holy wafer
found that strange. I hadn't
thought of it before then,
before the nun came down
through the ceiling to say
the Lord's Prayer, hadn't
thought of it before the girl
with rheumatic fever in the bed
next to mine asked that an offering
of camelias be made to the virgin
in the courtyard.

I could mention changelings
and omens. I would be at home
with prophecy. Even at Delphi
it was woman's work. I may speak
of a crossroads where the son
comes upon his father provided
I do not mention the crime, how
for years the boy slept in the bed
of his mother; how together
they began the generations,
their secret opened like an incision.

6

I mail packages, tidy a room,
open a window. I put a cup
on its shelf, seal a letter,
label a bottle. I do not mention
Brahms or Beethoven.

Even now I do not come fully forth
to these pages but creep out of bed
secretly like a nurse to her patient—
a lifelong training in the art
of the fragment, the art of the parcel,
the penny in a jar.

There is no one to blame here.
Only my life, thin on its leash,
domesticated beyond repair.

7

At night the dreams offer up the rags
of sleep—a rat bold as Lucretia leaves
its teeth marks in my wrist.

I trace out my genealogy, but the
letters are silent after all. I learn
only that I am man's *wom* or *wim*
or *wif*, the female portion of human.
But my history has its beginning
elsewhere. *Ish* and *Ishah*, woman
taken out of man, formed of his rib
as he slept. One flesh.
And before that

IV

Holding the House Down

Poem of the Mother

The heart goes out ahead
scouting for him
while I stay at home
keeping the fire,
holding the house down
around myself
like a skirt from the high wind.

The boy does not know
how my eye strains to make out
his small animal shape
swimming hard across the future
nor that I have strengthened myself
like the wood side of this house
for his benefit.

I stay still
so he can rail against me.
I stay at the fixed center of things
like a jar on its shelf
or the clock on the mantel
so when his time comes
he can leave me.

Winter Solstice

We must hurry
before the sun
leaves off
its coverage
of the bright places:
these days
are small
as thimbles.

Fire Eater,
swallow the flame
lest the heat
leak away
under a door.

Guard
in your frozen house,
catch a glimpse
of the thief
as he moves
across blue glass,
as he surprises you
like a lover
burning an impression
into your back,
taking it
all the way to bone.

At night
the stars
trained on the earth
like guns

fail to warm us:
their reconnaissance
took place
long ago.

We must hurry
our journeys,
storing what light
there is in bins,
in honeycombs
before the distance
draws us near,
before all
that bright opening
is shut down.

My Daughter's Dream

They are on a bus
The days
keep passing them

One night the driver announces
their destination
emptying them
at the gates of a camp

Adults to the left
Children to the right

She cannot decide

Now she moves to the left
She has read about this before
in a book with a torn cover
She could see
through all the pages

Children will be taken to training camps

I want to go there
she tells them
setting off down the road

They take her to the computer
which announces her birthday
Tomorrow she will be fifteen

Now she is seated at a table
They are singing to her

Exchange

FOR ELEUTHERIA AND KOULA

In the morning
the children tease me
giving me the word *melon*
for *shoe. Carpousi*,
they laugh, pointing
to my foot. I imagine
a great ripe cantaloupe.

In the evening
they take both
my hands and pull me
into the sky.
Tell us, they whisper
in Greek, what you call that,
they say, pointing
to a firmament so alive
with stars you cannot see
the dark places.

And tell us, they say,
pointing to the slice of moon,
golden as the cheese ripening
on the stone porches
under silken mulberry trees,
what it is named.

And I think to tell them
straight away, opening
my language to them
like a gift brightly wrapped,
though it is fair to say here
I was tempted to teach them

eyebrow in place of *star*, *button*
for *moon*, *scribble* for *sky*,
but I was leaving and I wouldn't
see them again,

so I unwrapped the words
and took them and opened their hands
and placed the words inside
so they could feel them
the way children in my country
feel the quivering body of a lightning bug
after it is caught, going off and on
that way in the warm small cave
of the palm.

Horseradish

FOR JANICE

It is ecumenical
to invite three Baptists
to the reform synagogue
for a Friday night service,
the pulpit stuffed
with clergy
like unleavened bread
beneath the ceremonial cloth,

but when you lift the cruciferous
horseradish from its bin—
hoary tuber with its ancient hairs
like a giant pubis
in your hand—
the greengrocer stares.

Safe, behind his white
enameled scale
he struggles to fix
the 20-cent sticker
to the dusty misshapen root.
The others in line
look at you
as though you have just unveiled
Pithecanthropus erectus
in their supermarket.

Nothing
compared to the bloody
shankbone of the lamb
you ask for next

of the nervous
well-instructed butcher
who accidentally hands you two,
his Paschal offering.

August

Perhaps it is true after all
I am their sister not mother
as you have always been saying

Perhaps I did not live
in these years tidy as socks
I was darning tidy as a kitchen

only yeast riding out its own dream of bread

and perhaps I never came here
at night to this room lifting
a child from its moist sleep

an act invented out of need

In what was my body rooted
here where all comes loose
like paper from its walls

where the very walls unfold
from the house

Shall I say to you
that the wood of the table
under my fingers is real

or the thunder partitioning the darkness

In the late clarity of August
I turn and turn a ring on my finger
as though it could keep in
this storm which my body prepares

Insomnia

While I bring myself
like a sentinel
through the three watches
of the night,
I continue to scan
the darkness
for signs of a sleep
that shuns me
as though I would injure it,
dreams I would harm
by entering their rooms again.

Were you awake
you would know
how your words
break away
from the smooth mouth
of sleep.
My thumb
pressed down at your wrist
corners a small heart
marking time
in the blood.

While each shadowy segment
lifts away behind me like a skin,
I measure the difference
between a white thread and a blue,
between wolf and dog.
The tea in its glass
on the table has grown cold
when I take note

of the first contractions
of light starting up
along the wall.

For This

But tell me, where is it you have traveled
in these four years? In sleep your death
rose up in my body, misshapen and familiar.

Here toward evening the trees start
to move down from the neighboring streets.
If I look away they take a step closer.

They lean in at my window. They bear
in their upper reaches the reliable stars.
Mother, is it your birth I was not able

to celebrate which I mark in these days?
Or a morning when two men came to take you
from a room which you had already abandoned?

Sweet skull which I shape between my fingers,
eyes which have gone wondering among the thoughts,
is it for this small share we come along this way?
For this jar of light we hold up to the breathing membrane?

V

Ritual

A Three-Course Meal for the New Year

This stalk of day-old bread
cannot move my soul
into the new year.
I am left behind again
in the synagogue
where the rabbi quotes
divorce statistics and heals
loneliness with transcendental
Jewish meditation.

I am left behind
holding the yellow ticket
which provides me
one unreserved seat
on the hard bench
of the sanctuary. I wave it
like a bee on a string,
afraid it will sting me,
afraid to let go.

Come to the synagogue,
the rabbi says,
but leave, he cautions,
with deliberate speed.
Four services going on
at the same time—
a little god spread thin
on next year's sandwich.

His fingers parted
in the cabalistic blessing,
I slip through the spaces

and come home, the new year
already at table before me.
The small husks of the days
of the old year hover in my room.
Later on I will take them out
to the river. And later
I will visit the grave
of my mother and offer praise
without knocking on wood
and take my first taste
of the sweet year.

Sacrifice

It is said
that for a man
the earth
is his mother.

But in Jerusalem
they say
that a man
takes the earth
as his wife.

That these fruits
of that earth—grape,
spikenard, cluster
of henna and green fig—
these are his offspring.

Remnants
brought to the table
innocent of the meal
as Isaac on his mountain,
as the ram of Abraham
at Moriah.

Instructions for the Messiah

Do not think
you must work signs
and miracles
or resurrect the dead.

It is sufficient
that you have diligently
studied the law.

We would ask of you
only the rebuilding
of the temple
and the gathering in
of the exiles.

These will define you

and nothing will seem changed.
Night will follow day
as it always has.

It was never for dominion
that we invented you
but only that we might
return to our houses.

Inside
we would know
the hidden things
of this world.

The Living House

There was a house
but it was not for sale
So I bought it
one hundred feet
above a creek
I bought this house
which was not for sale
and I stood
all day outside in the rain
of my house
which I could not own
and I gave it my name
and I brought to it
my life
And afterwards
they asked one another
they spoke in words
I could not understand
they said to one another
they whispered
in the rain
they insisted
And the house
which was not for sale
called out to them
I cannot be bought
my owner lives in me
And afterwards
I came there again
but my spirit refused
to go inside

Prayer for Endings

Let this vessel for water be perfect, and without
a broken place. Let its lip be even and unspouted;
we shall pour water from its edge.

And if there is no vessel, let us dip our hands
together into a stream and if the color of the water
has changed, let it be due to natural cause.

If the painter has hands which are covered with dye
or the butcher's with blood or the printer's with ink,
let these not be obstructions; let him wash with us.

And in the morning out of this golden theatre
where the shape of wood makes a parabola in the air
mapping out the curve of our life,

let us bury the other in us and all those years
which we opened like a text some faithful teacher
put into our hands for the first time

innocent of its lines and its intersections.
Let us close off in the morning the small valves of the heart
and all such doors to those rooms where we once lived.

After Theresienstadt*

FOR VERA

It does not matter;
it is only a word:

Maria Theresia's fortress,
a collection of stones.

If you move the letters around
like furniture—thick

and upholstered as great-aunts—
they will not complain.

Here is the word
which you entered in childhood

and here is the word
which took away

your breathing
and here is the word

grown wrinkled and dangerous
which labors to spit you

back into the world again.

*collection point for the gas chambers

Reunion

You have pasted up
green trees
in the right-hand corner
of this gray envelope
of land

You have sent in
prophets who are recruits
and after them
the dust
to dry up their words

I ask you
are these not reunions
even this stain of blood
which lies down
with the stone

Blessed Art Thou, No-One

No one kneads us again of earth and clay,
No one incants our dust.
No one.
Blessed art thou, No-One.

—PAUL CELAN

If I reach after you
into the darkness

will you stay put against my hand
or will I scrape against

the steady pulsing
of my own fingers

This day   held up
like a flag of warning

no-one made of words
soaked into the earth

stray words from the shrunken mouths
of those who sat down

in the forest
unlacing their shoes

Used up words
that we leaning

across a table wanted
to say to you

before the table
turned into a gun

before the chair fled
its house

If we attach the words
to our feet like a boot

will you walk on them
will they cry out

under you
like a woman

Will the faces of gravestones
call to you

when they are hammered into stairs
or set into roads

when the tanks run over
their names

Are you made of words no-one
shall I give you a name

or must your provisions
be metal and rope

or something to carry
these papers

so that you may cross
a border into your own life

VI

The Way Out

Letting the Plants Die

This one's gone to straw   I cannot say
I'm sorry   and this one on the piano
is getting darker and stiff   I hardly look

but they leave their telltale signs
everywhere   the dry crisp leaves
on the window sill   the tendrils
hardened around the pillows of the sofa
the aphids vanished into the woodwork

The avocado is on its side   the Swedish
ivy I started from a cutting   the asparagus
fern spreading up the wall   daring to bloom
in winter

I am letting them die   glad to be free
of mist sprays and fertilizers   fish
emulsion I keep meaning to buy
free of double wavy blossoms   all
they ever had to offer

I hardly think of them anymore
walking through these rooms   but
sometimes I remember a man in a Greek
novel I was once reading   hovering
utterly naked behind his enormous
overgrown philodendron

The other side of the coin

How Metaphor Can Save Your Life

You are drowning.
Someone throws you an inflatable sunset
which momentarily distracts you
from the sinking ship, the cramp
in your left leg, the barracuda
who has just sidled up next to you.
You forget that you do not know
how to swim. Your thrashing about,
your simulated swimming strokes
bring out the Coast Guard.

You find a small tumor
behind your left earlobe.
The dark cloud of cancer descends
just as the doctor tells you
you have Dutch elm disease
and need to wash more frequently
behind your ears.

You have just lost your job.
You have no money in the bank.
EAT LOVE, someone has written
on the bulletin board at the unemployment
office. A man proposes on the hard bench.
You accept and live happily
ever afterword.

You are on an airplane.
Suddenly it hits an air pocket and drops
a thousand feet into a cloud bank.
You climb out of the window. You have always
wanted to touch a cloud. You hold yourself

aloft by doing yoga. Soon your parachute
opens. You sail safely through a grove
of redwood trees, your arms full
of cumulonimbus towers from the cloud bank.
You learn that the Dow Jones is up.

In Bed

Jewish extremities—cold
hands and cold feet,
all that long history
stretching back before Christ
and the Magi
or going forth into who knows what
new calamity.

Why do you have such cold hands?
he wants to know.

It's the history, I say to him
while he blows on my fingers,
while he prevents me from wrapping cold
around his body.
The history blowing through these rooms,
I tell him. The old story of exile
and assassination.

Why are your toes so cold? he says,
cradling my feet in his own.

The history, I reiterate, warming
to this dialectic. The way the history
goes from one desert to another. Or stalls,
I think to myself, in some cozy doctrine
certain as the yellow-backed antelope
bedded down in straw, the afternoon sun
encircling her.

Holes

There are holes
making themselves larger
in my body.

What I ingest
of the world
adds
to the excavation:

my friend who asks
if I cannot hear
the sounds her bones make
breaking through her skin,
the small lip sounds
coming up
through her skirt;
hostages,
new generation missiles,
mutations
which irradiate
the moist wall
of this catacomb.

Meanwhile
the holes
in my body
deepen
to windows.

Soon the principal investigator
will be able to see
the archaeological site
from the outside.

Speech Warts

Fetch me a red flower from that meadow,
says Ludwig. I look at him. Which shade
of red? What species of flower? And on
what green stalk? He stares back at me.
And above all, I say to him, which meadow?
He is silent. How shall I get there with-
out losing the flower, the one he has
imagined? I take a sheet from my left
pocket which contains the shapes of all
English and American flowers. I take a
glass prism from my right pocket. Now I
march up to the nearest meadow and compare
real flowers with my chart of flower
shapes. I pass a ray of sunlight through
my prism and produce a color band which
I compare with the colors of flowers. But
the flowers in the meadow are in foreign
languages: Sprechenvorts! Gehimmelhymen-
optera! they shout at me. Λουλούδια, they
continue to berate me, this time in Greek,
mocking my shape grilles, my color bands.
What next? I ask him. Fetch me the meadow,
he says. Be quick about it. I come back,
my arms full. I can barely walk under the
weight of sumac, wild barley, their names
heavy in Russian, Serbo-Croatian, various
Indo-European tongues. My face is a sheath
of red flowers. No the one I had imagined,
he tells me. Not that one, he repeats.
Nowhere to be found in the vast meadow you
have brought me. I set down the meadow
before him. I take a sheet of paper from my

hip pocket. I write on it: A RED FLOWER FROM THAT MEADOW, and I attach it to a stick which I set upright, waving, in the center of the meadow. That one, Ludwig whispers gratefully. That is the one.

Appeasing a River

from a spoken line by Bill Stafford

We gave the river a girl.
In winter. The blades
of her skates were sharp.
The thin edge of ice

took her to water. We
thought it ended there.
But at night in a car
Marianne skipped fence

and tree like a stone
on water and came into it
upside down and unconscious.
Water rose up to the door

handle. Its cold brought her
around in time and she
floated out. We did not know
how to save the others.

On a Sunday at St. Mary's
the boys made a cradle
of their hands and carried
the bodies down the narrow

aisle. We went slower
down that street by the river.
Until little by little
we hurried the town again.

The Town

You go cautiously
around the past, circling it
or taking rooms
miles from it
still keeping it in view.

Or walking the main street
at night when the townsmen
are sleeping—coming back,
oh coming back only then
and alone so that nothing disturbs
your view of it, no voice
comes correcting it saying:

It went like this

He was clubfooted; they called him
Fortunato, one of five brothers.
How often he stood warming himself
by the entryway in spring,
guarding his part of that town.

So the self stands in its town
no smaller than you remember it,
idling there
like Fortunato in his doorway,
saying:

It went like this

You walk out, leaving it
once and for all, saying you won't

be back. You tell them
and they look at you wanting
to leave themselves and not quite
believing your version of their lives,

knowing all the while
how you will dream of them,
how you will take them
at last from their doorways
and bring them along with you,
how they will be altered
by the way you see them.

If You Are Willing

This language   You once owned it
It can be opened again   You need
only untie the words   letting the frayed edges
fall away   and the sounds will take up residence
again on your tongue   For isn't it so that
words bring their own genealogies
offering their version of this world

And you reach in   taking them
between your fingers   as you did
in childhood the invented creatures you pocketed
who ate their way all night
through your own terrible loneliness

Kneeling into the darkness let
what is without form materialize
in you   These broken pieces
hands that will come to you there
Dark going out to meet dark
or some thread pulling in
the silence   drawing you on
And you move in it like water
Your body swims out to it if you are willing
enough and the bright shapes take form
opening inside you

The Traveler

FOR LEN RANDOLPH

Behind you
the road
gathers itself
trying to follow
though its eye
cannot make you out
clearly now
for your feet
are already
in motion
In front of you
the road unfurls
its flag
sickle and star
in one background
Departure
and arrival
are made
of the same cloth
The past
with its one room
and its words
written
into the walls
engraved
on our tongues
lest we forget
someone
who wished us well
or a word
by which we lived
The future

which we unravel
as we go
pulling it along
behind us
or tugging at it
as we approach
for some sign
for the answering quiver
along the thread
as we turn
to greet ourselves

The Goodbye

This endsaying—moon pried loose
by grave force, pulled
out of earth's sweet atmosphere—
this has been formulated in every place.
In each text it is known.

At birth, the broken covenant
with before—parting from it hand
over hand along the dark way,
or valve closing
on its nine month work—breath
in the place of blood.

Or in sleep—it rises
like a ghostly glacier
bounded on each side
by consciousness;
it calls us
and we go at night
to that kindly absence—
sealed ark
bearing us toward morning.

Or in the sudden heat of love
when the body senses the cold deeply
like breathing in.
The Goodbye—it is well known.
What more to say of it?

We play it back—old film,
refugees in our torn ships, sailing
the bruised distance.

We walk upright on this earth
for our allotted time. Love,
we pass you as before. Yet
this passing has the shape
of farewell.

Other Titles in the Contemporary Poetry Series

James Applewhite, *Statues of the Grass*
Susan Astor, *Dame*
D. C. Berry, *Saigon Cemetery*
Hayden Carruth, *The Bloomingdale Papers*
Tony Connor, *New and Selected Poems*
Franz Douskey, *Rowing Across the Dark*
John Engels, *Vivaldi in Early Fall*
Brendan Galvin, *Atlantic Flyway*
Michael Heffernan, *The Cry of Oliver Hardy*
Philip Legler, *The Intruder*
Jayanta Mahapatra, *A Rain of Rites*
Charles Martin, *Room for Error*
Marion Montgomery, *The Gull and Other Georgia Scenes*
John Ower, *Legendary Acts*
Bin Ramke, *White Monkeys*
Paul Ramsey, *No Running on the Boardwalk*
Vern Rutsala, *The Journey Begins*
Laurie Sheck, *Amaranth*
Paul Smyth, *Conversions*
Marcia Southwick, *The Night Won't Save Anyone*
Barry Spacks, *Imagining a Unicorn*
Mary Swander, *Succession*